A Photographer at the Aldeburgh Festival

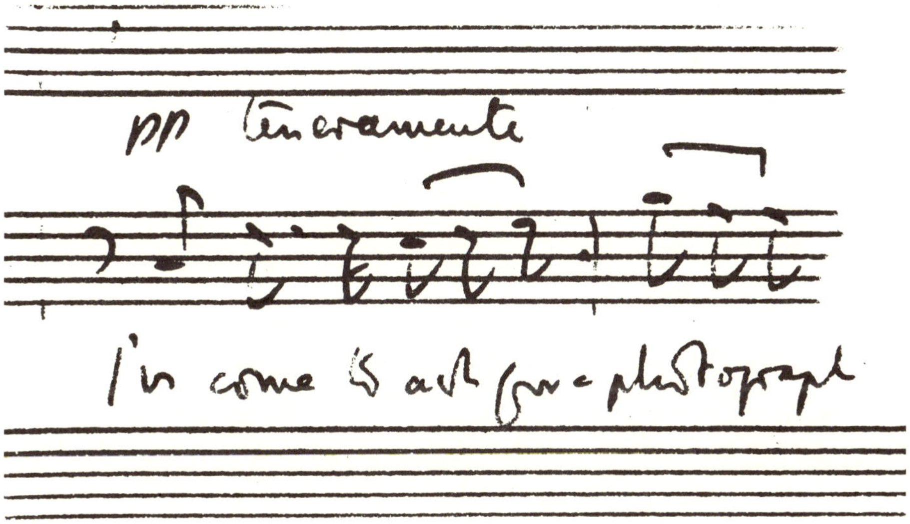

Britten's original manuscript

'I've come to ask
For a photograph . . .'
Police Superintendent Budd in *Albert Herring*, 1947.

'"Why not," said Peter Pears (in 1947), "make our own Festival? A modest Festival with a few concerts given by friends? Why not have an Aldeburgh Festival?"'

– Eric Crozier.

'. . . the quality of the Aldeburgh Festival, which is not so much a series of performances as a gathering of friends – on both sides of the footlights. The performances are, as a matter of fact, of the very highest standard; but everybody seems to be doing it for fun.'
– Bernard Levin, *The Times*, 28 June 1974.

'A festival should be festive. And it must possess something which is distinctive and which could not be so well presented elsewhere.'
– E. M. Forster, Aldeburgh, 1948.

'Exactly,' wrote Robert Commanday, the greatly respected music critic of *The San Francisco Chronicle*, after quoting E. M. Forster, and describing his own first visit to the Festival in 1988. 'Unquestionably, the Aldeburgh Festival represents a personal monument to Britten's and Pears' careers and artistic ideals. With the passing of Britten and then Pears, the affection for them and the support of what they started have not lessened . . . By varying its concert sites, the Aldeburgh Festival affords the visitor the chance to experience the unique feeling of the coastal area of Suffolk . . . E. M. Forster was right and Aldeburgh meets his definition. It's festive, it's distinctive . . .'

To all our friends at the Aldeburgh Festival and in affectionate and grateful memory of Ben, Imo and Peter

Fireworks at Framlingham: Peter Pears' birthday celebrations, 1975.

A Photographer at
THE ALDEBURGH FESTIVAL

NIGEL LUCKHURST

Arranged and Introduced by

John Amis, Richard Butt and Norman Scarfe

The Alastair Press

Published by
The Alastair Press
2 Hatter Street
Bury St Edmunds
Suffolk

First published in 1990

ISBN 1 870567 56 0

Book designer: Stephen du Sautoy

Front cover: Snape Maltings
Back cover: Norman Scarfe, John Amis and Richard Butt on Crag Path.
Endpapers: Aldeburgh beach: the *Grimes* element: where it all begins. Peter Pears as Aschenbach on the deserted beach at the Lido in *Death in Venice*, towards the end.

Photoset by Rowland Phototypesetting Limited,
Bury St Edmunds, Suffolk
Printed in Great Britain by
St Edmundsbury Press Limited,
Bury St Edmunds, Suffolk

Three authors on the steps of the courtroom of Aldeburgh Moot Hall – Norman Scarfe, Richard Butt and John Amis

Putting you in the Pictures
John Amis

Aldeburgh is a hundred miles from London on the East Anglian coast facing what used to be called the German Ocean, a small seaside place north of Suffolk's county town, Ipswich, and south of the port of Lowestoft where Benjamin Britten was born on 22nd November 1913. Most of his life was spent in Suffolk: *Peter Grimes* was written in the Old Mill, Snape; in 1947 Britten and his singer companion Peter Pears moved into Crag House, Crabbe Street, Aldeburgh. The first Festival took place in June 1948. In 1957 they moved inland, to the Red House on the outskirts of Aldeburgh, at the edge of the golfcourse. Later they acquired another small house at Horham, midway between Framlingham and Diss, for interludes of greater peace and quiet, but the Red House was their main dwelling place. Britten died there in December, 1976, Pears in April, 1986.

For the first nineteen years the two chief venues of the Festival were the Parish Church and the Jubilee Hall in Aldeburgh, neither of them large. Even by the time the Hall had been rebuilt in 1960 it could still not hold more than 350 seats. Fortunately the 19th-century Malting-house in the nearby village of Snape (in sight of Britten's *Grimes* mill) became available; it was converted into an 850-seater multi-purpose concert-hall and open-stage auditorium. It was opened in time for the 1967 festival, burnt out on the opening night of the 1969 festival and rebuilt with astonishing speed to be ready for the 1970 session. From 1977 the Maltings also housed the Britten–Pears School for Advanced Studies. The acoustics of the Maltings are perfect, its interior plain but pleasing, its situation idyllic. Britten once remarked that it was the only concert-hall in the world where you could walk out in the interval and see a red-shank.

Nigel Luckhurst became photographer to the Festival when it was 26 years old. In its infancy the organising body was the English Opera Group, formed to look after performances of *The Rape of Lucretia* and *Albert Herring* premièred at Glyndebourne in 1946 and 1947. Motoring back across Europe after an arduous and unrewarding tour Peter asked why they didn't start their own festival at home. The Group effectively consisted of BB and PP (as we shall often call them from now on), together with John Piper, the painter who designed seven Britten operas and a ballet, Joan Cross who created five major roles for the composer and Eric Crozier who wrote the librettos for two Britten operas and produced a third. Since the designer's wife, Myfanwy, wrote three of Ben's librettos, and Mrs Crozier/Nancy Evans created three major roles, it can be inferred that Britten liked to keep his activities within a kind of artistic family.

Of course Britten often had to venture out into the rest of the world but was always glad to get back home to compose; as often as not, to compose something for the next festival. He wrote *Saint Nicolas* for the first festival, *Phaedra* for the last that he attended, and no less than twenty-four other works premièred at the Festival between 1948 and 1976, including *The Little Sweep*, *Noye's Fludde*, *A Midsummer Night's Dream* and the three Church-Parables. In the pre-Maltings years Copland, Kodàly, Poulenc, Brain and Ferrier took part; BB and PP performed countless times in each and every festival. How could such a festival not be truly and uniquely worthy of the name? No other could boast such a roster of names and premières.

There were, naturally, complaints of cliques and references to Bayreuth; in the former case with some justification. Britten was hyper-sensitive to any sort of criticism so that he tended, understandably, to work with people he knew and found reliable and sympathetic. With such an unbelievable workload it could scarcely have been otherwise. As for the comparison with Bayreuth where Wagner's was the only music played (give or take a ceremonial Beethoven Ninth Symphony), a glance at the list of music performed at the Festival up to the year 1987 reveals that, beside the 2¼ pages devoted to the works of Britten, there are 74¾ pages devoted to the works of other composers, including well over a hundred premières.

So, what happened specifically in the Luckhurst years, 1974–1978? The photos and captions tell most, but here is a very select list of information and events that may help you to get your bearings:

1975 Patron: the Queen Mother; President: the Countess of Cranbrook; Artistic Directors: BB, PP, Imogen Holst, Philip Ledger, Colin Graham, Steuart Bedford; General Manager: William Servaes; Secretary: Keith Cable. Première of the folk-song suite *A Time There Was* by Britten, who attended the concert but was, since his heart operation in 1973, unable to play or conduct. Performances of *Death in Venice*.

1976 Rostropovich Family concert: Mstislav, Galina, Olga and Elena. BB's operetta *Paul Bunyan* given first UK staging. His cantata *Phaedra* premièred by its dedicatee, Janet Baker. The composer was present but died in December, 12 days after his 63rd birthday. North Sea very grey that day.

1977 Purcell's *The Fairy Queen* staged. Début of Snape Maltings Training Orchestra.

1978 Rostropovich joins Artistic Directors, Imogen Holst becomes Emeritus.

1979 Orford performances of *Curlew River* and *The Burning Fiery Furnace*. Britten-Pears School stages *Eugene Onegin* conducted by Rostropovich. *The Martyrdom of St. Magnus* by P. Maxwell Davies staged.

1980 *A Midsummer Night's Dream*. Last festival at which PP sang.

1981 *The Prodigal Son*. Rostropovich. Rozhdestvensky.

1982 Kent Opera stages BB's version of *The Beggar's Opera*. William Walton. Isaac Stern. Hugues Cuénod.

1983 BB–PP School stages *The Turn of the Screw*. Lutoslawski at 70. Berkeley at 80. Artistic directors joined by Murray Perahia and John Shirley-Quirk, Oliver Knussen, and Simon Rattle who conducts *War Requiem* at Bury. Horszowski's Aldeburgh début.

1984 *Owen Wingrave*. Imogen Holst died on 9th March truly one of music's hand-maidens, a quite exceptional person and musician.

1985 *Rodelinda*. Henri Dutilleux composer-in-residence.

1986 *Albert Herring*. Act III of *Parsifal*/Goodall. Last Amadeus Concert. Hans Werner Henze composer-in-residence. Peter Pears died on 6th April.

1987 *Rape of Lucretia*. Lukas Foss composer-in-residence.

1988 U.S. production of *Paul Bunyan*. Tchaikovsky's *Iolanta*. György Kurtàg. Alfred Schnittke composer-in-residence.

By this time the title of President of the Festival had been handed on to The Princess of Hesse and the Rhine. Princess Margaret (she is a Geddes) and her late husband Prince Ludwig of Hesse had initiated the Hesse Student Scheme which enabled young people to come to the Festival each year, providing some particularly intelligent faces and ears in the audience and helping with minor tasks like putting up music stands on the stage and programme leaflets on the seats, tasks that Imo and Ben had found themselves doing in earlier years.

Having relinquished in 1988 the task of photographing the Festival, Nigel Luckhurst gave a retrospective exhibition in 1989 in the Royal British Legion Hall, Aldeburgh. The three scribes of this book, unbeknownst to each other, wrote almost by the same post to Nigel, suggesting that a book of his Festival photographs was imperative. He replied by putting us in touch with each other, exhorting us to get on with it and, hey presto!, here is the book, thanks to the encouragement of Virginia Caldwell and John Jacob of the Festival, Stephen and Alison du Sautoy, the publishers, and a benevolent Trust Fund.

Nigel is not to be blamed for the selection of the photographs nor the captions. On the other hand it was he who had selected the three or four hundred that we initially looked at, explaining to us that those were only the top of an ocean of over 15,000 negatives. For the book we decided to eschew chronology and to feel our way, occasionally by subject but more often following our collective noses and seeing what went with what. No picture is included just because the person or subject was important; the criterion was the photograph itself. Anyway, the difficulty was not what to put in . . .

Taking Stock
Richard Butt

It has been rather like stock taking! Not as we would in Mrs Herring's shop in Loxford, but in a musical Aladdin's cave.

We have looked at hundreds of Nigel Luckhurst's Festival pictures, a joy in itself, and for me recalling the wonderful musical experiences of thirty Festivals; for twenty-six of them broadcasting and recording for the BBC, a task that often took me into the heart of events, like Nigel with his camera, trying not to get in the way but always alert to a performer's need for another pair of ears to consider points of balance or any other difficulty that might present itself. While much has changed and developed during that time I think a great deal of the original spirit remains.

The musical spirit stemmed in the first place from the 'enthusiasms' of the Founders and Artistic Directors. Mozart and Schubert, those unforgettable performances of 'Die schöne Müllerin' and 'Winterreise', and the later Viennese, Mahler and Berg. Britten's devotion to the neglected Schumann with performances of the *Scenes from Faust* and *Manfred* and the recitals of the vocal chamber music. Peter Pears' skill as the Evangelist in the Bach Passions must have led him to Heinrich Schütz. In Bach and Purcell they were joined by Imogen Holst whose work as editor and performer opened the doors for many of us to the riches of the pre-Baroque repertoire. Nor should we forget Percy Grainger!

And then in a situation lacking a proper theatre, it has always been a marvel of resourcefulness and determination that there have been regular operatic productions including new operas by Berkeley, Birtwistle, Crosse, Maxwell Davies, Musgrave and Williamson, as well as many of Britten's theatre works, from *Paul Bunyan* to *Death in Venice*. Outstanding among the productions have been the 1979 *Onegin* conducted by Rostropovich, and Janet Baker in Purcell's *Dido and Aeneas* in 1974, the year of the Holst centenary when we heard his Choral Symphony (the major victim of the 1969 fire) and a memorable double bill of *Savitri* and *The Wandering Scholar*. It was also the year when Norrington's Schütz Choir sang Bach and he conducted *Manfred*; David Munrow set our feet tapping with Dance Music of Four Centuries played by his Early Music Consort augmented to almost symphonic proportions. Imogen Holst wrote and lectured about her father – what a wonderful lecturer! Two years later, she spoke on Editing other people's music. As a result of this I spent a whole day with her discussing Bach's B minor Mass, page by page. Her enthusiasm, perception and humility will never be forgotten. There was always a kind of divine clarity about those three great musicians, Britten, Pears and Holst at work in the clear light of East Anglia. Like Constable and the Norwich School of painters, and Nigel Luckhurst too!

Personal friendships have attracted musicians of international distinction to the Festival, often to play music specially written for them. One thinks of the Cello Symphony and the Three Suites for Rostropovich and 'The Poet's Echo' for his wife, Galina Vishnevskaya. The Blake 'Songs and Proverbs' for Dietrich Fischer-Dieskau. Special links have been forged with Richter and Clifford Curzon. Murray Perahia came to play and stayed to become an Artistic Director. Aldeburgh is a place you have to come back to, Julian Bream has been coming back for years, and so have Janet Baker, Heather Harper, John Shirley-Quirk, and the conductor and harpsichordist George Malcolm, whose recitals of Scarlatti and Couperin and his performance of Bach's Goldberg Variations have been among the high points of the Festivals.

In recent years the work of the Britten-Pears School, its orchestra and the opera class have made important contributions to the concerts, along with the regular involvement of many other young, new composers, players and singers. That is a continuing part of the Festival's spirit. So, we hope you will combine your delight in Nigel Luckhurst's pictures with your own memories of the music, and perhaps return to the old programme books which, like the Festival itself, should be enjoyed and cherished for being handsomely made, and filled with imagination and quality.

The Aldeburgh Country

Norman Scarfe

Aldeburgh, with the fishermen's working boats perched along its pebbly beach and the wide estuary winding past, from Snape and Iken down to Sudbourne and Orford and finally out into the North Sea, is Crabbe's country; in the way that East Bergholt, Dedham and the Stour valley are Constable's country. Ronald Duncan, who wrote the libretto of *The Rape of Lucretia* for Britten, said that 'Crabbe did for Aldeburgh what Jane Austen did for Bath'. 'And,' one might add, 'what Guy de Maupassant, one of whose stories suggested *Albert Herring*, did for Fécamp and thereabouts.' Crabbe's talents were very much those of a novelist or short-story writer. He rather pointedly wrote this line:

'As Truth will paint it, and as Bards will not.'

Not for nothing is his lively bust by the local sculptor Thurlow (1847, in Aldeburgh parish church) labelled: 'The poet of nature and truth'.

Jane Austen apparently averred that she could fancy being Mrs Crabbe. (Could it, conceivably, have worked?) He lived out his last years in a Wiltshire rectory, nearer her country than his own. Yet, as E. M. Forster saw,

> 'he never escaped from Aldeburgh in the spirit, and it was the making of him as a poet. Even when he is writing of other things, there steals again and again into his verse the sea, the estuary, the flat Suffolk coast, and local meannesses, and an odour of brine and dirt – tempered occasionally with the scent of flowers'.
>
> 'On the wide heath, or in the flow'ry vale,
> We scent the vapours of the sea-borne gale', etc.

Forster's talk about George Crabbe was printed in *The Listener* in 1942. It showed how effectively Crabbe linked the landscape of his most powerful poem, *The Borough* (1810), with the mood, the psychology, of the characters in the poem – most notably in the story of 'Peter Grimes', a callous fisherman whose brutal use of his solitary apprentices alienated the whole borough. There was an actual original for Grimes, called Tom Brown. His horrifying life and death sparked the most vivid of Crabbe's verse-tales, and in turn illuminated Forster's broadcast, which was nostalgically powerful enough to pull Britten and Pears back home from America in 1942. Before the war, Britten had bought a converted post-windmill overlooking Snape maltings. In it the great opera was written, ready for production in 1945.

From then on, Crabbe's country became also, indeed more famously, Britten's country. The storm, in Act I of *Peter Grimes*, has driven furiously through opera houses all across the world; thrilling and implacable as the elements that have eroded half the town of Aldeburgh. When I hear Grimes sing: 'I am native rooted here by familiar fields, marsh and sand, ordinary streets, prevailing wind,' I know what he is singing, for, like Grimes, I am a native, rooted hereabouts, as Britten was, a little way up the coast at Lowestoft; and as Kenneth Clark (Lord Clark) was, who spent the first fifteen years of his life based at Sudbourne Hall on 'the other side of the Alde'. He once wrote:

> 'Others are better qualified than I am to understand the technical mastery of Ben's music; but in so far as it takes some of its colouring from the sea, and the skies and marshes of East Suffolk, I can claim to be an initiate. Grimes and Herring are my compatriots. To sit in Orford church, where I had spent so many hours of my childhood dutifully awaiting some spark of divine fire, and then to receive it at last in the performance of *Noye's Fludde*, was an overwhelming experience.'

This is how the Aldeburgh country has taken shape, a country infused with the slightly morose, occasionally smiling but sardonic, disillusioned spirit of Crabbe's verse-views, transformed by the greater genius of Britten and all his friends and musical interpreters; the singers, Peter Pears above all; the designers, and the unending procession of performers drawn to his country by Britten's magic – like the enchanted processions of God's creatures advancing with proper confidence and hope into Noye's Ark.

I have long been bemused by the knowledge that Queen Elizabeth I's friend Robert Dudley's actors played in Aldeburgh church in the June of 1573, two days after they had performed down the road in Ipswich. There seems a good chance that Shakespeare himself played here late in the summer of 1595, the year after *A Midsummer Night's Dream* was written; for his company certainly played in Ipswich that year. As historians too often find in their researches, a gap occurs that year in Aldeburgh's records: it would.

But in these recent years of the Aldeburgh Festival, there is no shortage of records, and among the most delightful are these made by Nigel Luckhurst. They show us all over Aldeburgh itself, afoot and at leisure, and within that broad-aisled early Tudor church, in the Baptist chapel, in various galleries and in the cinema. They show the Festival-visitors safely over the Meare at Thorpeness, and facing the distractions of the Sailors' Path to Snape; in, and outside, the Maltings there, of course, and in churches much further afield – in Orford and Framlingham, Southwold and Blythburgh (unforgettably hospitable in days when there was no Maltings concert-hall); and, further west, in Hadleigh and Bury. Houses, too, shown here as part of the Aldeburgh country, range across from nearby Blackheath (Friston) and Loudham (near Wickham Market) to Ickworth House, Long Melford Hall and even Heveningham Hall.

When an Audience Survey was made in 1984, it showed that, fairly naturally, about half the Festival audiences came from round about, in East Anglia. The Survey concluded: 'It is the atmosphere, surroundings and location of the Festival that Festival-goers find most attractive; of course, the quality of performance and wide variety of the programme also play a major part in their enjoyment.' The Aldeburgh country has a lot to answer for, and a very great deal to live up to.

Picture Preface

Nigel Luckhurst

My first visit to Snape was for the dress rehearsal of *Death in Venice* in June 1973. The photographs I took on that occasion were well received and led to commissions to photograph productions in 1974. The then general manager, Bill Servaes, agreed to let me photograph the 1975 Festival, giving me free rein to move backstage as I wanted. The majority of the photographs of this festival were taken with a Hasselblad camera and a few with a Leica. The following year and every subsequent year this situation was reversed as the Leica was much more suited to my way of working.

Whenever possible I prefer to use available light to preserve the atmosphere and to cause as little inconvenience as possible to the subject. In that way I tend to be ignored – either the subjects do not notice me or else it is so dark that they do not believe it is possible to photograph at all without flash! It is in this situation that the Leica is particularly superb, the lenses seeming to have a great capacity to use what little light there is to create pictures.

Since 1985 I have also used Leica reflex cameras for both colour and monochrome. My personal preference is for monochrome – it seems to impart more of a timeless appeal to pictures, especially those of people and I have control over the result in the darkroom. Each festival means approximately 50 rolls of 35mm film, mostly Ilford HP5. The cameras used have been: Hasselblad 500 c/M & ELM, Leica M2 & M3 rangefinder and R3 & R4S reflex. Hasselblad lenses have ranged from 50mm to 350mm and the Leica from 21mm to 280mm.

I must record my thanks to some of the people who have been of great help and tolerance – if I miss anyone I apologise in advance. Bill Servaes and Jenni Vaulkhard gave me the opportunity in the first place and for that I am very grateful. Keith Cable and all the office staff. Bill and Jean Roberts and Pam Denny for their many kindnesses. Bob and Doris Ling for the tea, coffee and biscuits as well as their company. All the BBC teams, both Radio 3 and Transcription, have tolerated my presence both on stage during rehearsals and in their recording areas and who have never excluded me from either a rehearsal or live transmission. Even the announcers have not been put off by my camera appearing as they were about to broadcast!

It has never ceased to surprise me how helpful the vast majority of the performers have been. To be allowed, as a complete stranger, into what is quite often their only rehearsal before a concert is quite a privilege. Very rarely have I been refused.

My final thanks go to Norman Scarfe, Richard Butt and John Amis without whom this book would not have appeared, and particular thanks to my family, Jeanette, Emily and Alison. With special thanks to my mother, who allowed me to disrupt her kitchen and take over her garage before I had a darkroom, and still wishes I would get a proper job.

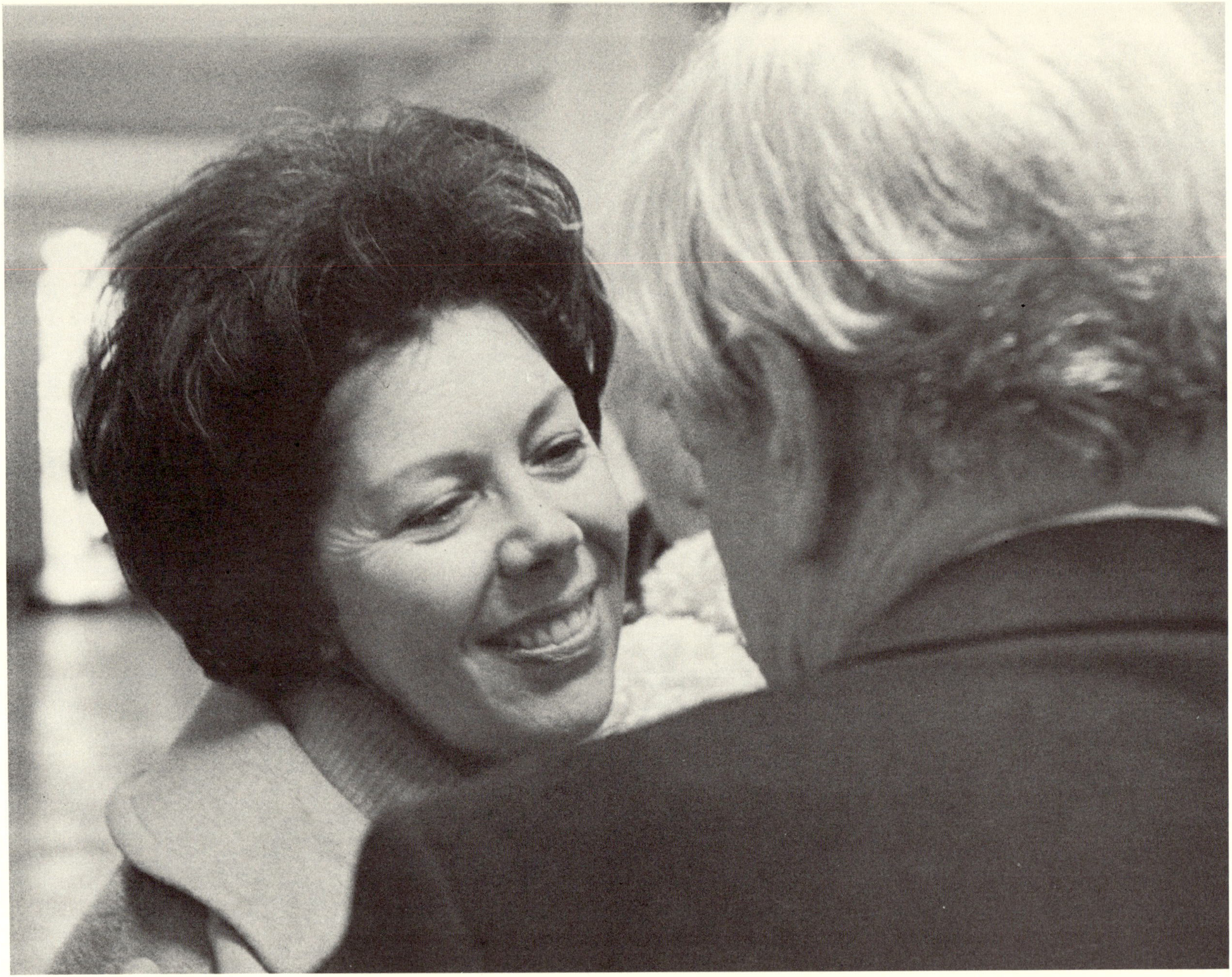

Peter Pears with Janet Baker. After a performance of Britten's *Phaedra*, 1977.

Patrick Garland, theatrical producer, and Benjamin Britten during Britten's last Festival, 1976.

Keith Cable receiving a present from Princess Margaret of Hesse for his work for the Hesse students. On the left, Frank E. Taplin, a Director of the American Friends of the Festival, 1985.

David Hockney visited the Red House in 1980, commissioned to draw Peter Pears for his 70th birthday. The portrait of Benjamin Britten is by Henry Lamb.

The Princess of Hesse and Peter Pears with composers Peter Paul Nash and Oliver Knussen, one of the Artistic Directors, 1985.

Open Day at the Britten-Pears Library, adjoining the Red House: the working collection of manuscripts, books, music and recordings built up during their lifetime. To this, relevant material is still being added. Many other composers and performers are represented. (Architect: Peter Collymore, 1963.) 1986.

Peter Pears and George ('Dadie') Rylands, Fellow of King's, friend of Lytton Strachey and Peggy Ashcroft, lifelong pundit of diction and drama, promoter and patron of the stage. Took part in the Maltings *Manfred*, 1974. Here he has just produced his programme about E. M. Forster, 1979.

The legendary pianist, Mieczyslaw Horszowski (born 1892), made his Aldeburgh début in 1983. 1985.

The Princess of Hesse and the great cellist, Mstislav Rostropovich, at the 1986 Festival party.

Herbert ('Bert') Pearce, of Steinways; in charge of the keyboards for many Festivals. 1977.

The Schubertians, the men's chamber choir from Santa Barbara, University of Los Angeles, with their Director, Carl Zytowski, 1979.

Donald Mitchell and Isador Caplan. DM, writer, administrator, friend and publisher of Benjamin Britten, executor of his estate, now trustee of the B-P Foundation and the Britten–Pears Library; an early admirer of the composer and specialist writer on his music and life; editing Britten's letters; on Aldeburgh Council since 1977, also in charge of academic studies at the Britten–Pears School for Advanced Musical Studies, Snape. *The Burning Fiery Furnace* is dedicated to Donald and his wife, Kathleen. IC looked after the legal affairs of BB and has been adviser to the Festival since 1961; also an executor of the estate and as such responsible for the innovatory arrangement enabling Britten's manuscripts to be accepted in lieu of death duties *and* remain in Aldeburgh at the Britten–Pears Library; he and his wife Joan were intimate friends of the composer, who dedicated to them his opera *Owen Wingrave*. 1980.

The Finchley Children's Music Group in Britten's *The Golden Vanity*, 1986.

Imogen Holst and William Servaes, the gifted general manager/administrator of the Festivals, 1972–80. 'Daughter of the Planets' she was sometimes called; she spent her life in the service of music and musicians: teacher, composer, conductor, writer, administrator, biographer of her father Gustav and cataloguer/editor of his work: amanuensis for 13 years to Benjamin Britten, and joint dedicatee of his ballet *The Prince of the Pagodas*, Artistic Director of the Festival 1956–77 (also its most photogenic character); she lived for 30 years in Aldeburgh and died there in 1984. 1980.

Myfanwy and John Piper with Basil Coleman at a rehearsal of *Owen Wingrave* in the Maltings. BB had three librettos from Myfanwy, one ballet and seven operas designed by John: no wonder they were honoured and beloved friends of BB. And Basil too, who produced the premières of three big Britten operas and the *Little Sweep*. 1984.

Imogen Holst listening to the balance. A young quartet rehearses Haydn in Aldeburgh parish church, 1978.

The Britten–Pears School were presenting *The Turn of the Screw*. Evoking the original 1954 production, Donald Mitchell chairs a symposium of original creators. Left to right: Pears (Quint), Myfanwy Piper (librettist), Joan Cross (Mrs Grose), Basil Coleman (producer), John Piper (designer). BB and PP's private collection of Piper's work was displayed here round the Peter Pears Gallery, Aldeburgh. 1983.

Albert Herring, B–P School's production, 1986. Albert, defiant after his profligate pub-crawl, is being roundly castigated by Loxford society: Cast no. 2: Gerard O'Beirne (Albert); Margaret Maguire (Lady Billows). 1986.

Members of the 1986 symposium on *Albert Herring* – Norman Lumsden (Superintendent Budd), Roy Ashton (Mr Upfold), Nancy Evans (Nancy), and David Spenser (Harry) – who sang in the first performances in 1947 at Glyndebourne. 1986.

Members of the Royal Shakespeare Company brought *The Hollow Crown* to the Maltings. Could the Plough and Sail, next door, compete with the Boar's Head tavern in Eastcheap? From Snape quay here, at the head of the estuary, grain produced by the local *ploughs* used to be shipped round the coast by barges under *sail* (see p. 61). 1982.

Snape Maltings. Doris Ling, Sylvia and Horace Smith behind the bar entertaining Simon and Irène Loftus, 1980.

The actors Anton Rodgers and Nicola Paget having their soles skinned on Aldeburgh beach. 1976.

John Burrell, of a well-established family of Aldeburgh fishermen. E. M. Forster often stayed with another Burrell, John's brother Billy, and his wife Barbara. 1976.

Gillian Weir, distinguished organist. The poet Crabbe's bust shares the 'organ chamber' in Aldeburgh parish church: see introduction, p. 9. 1982.

Jenni Vaulkhard and Norman Del Mar outside the Jubilee Hall, 1978. JV helped the Aldeburgh Foundation for many years, especially 1974–9 when she was Concert Administrator looking after events, concerts and artists. NDM in 1949 directed the première of *Let's Make an Opera*; conducted many symphony concerts and the English Opera Group in *Albert Herring*, *The Rape of Lucretia*, *The Beggar's Opera* and *Love in a Village*; he and his wife Pauline often combine visits to the Festival with seeing Joan Cross at her home in Aldeburgh.

A Jubilee Hall audience, 1984.

Aldeburgh Town Walk. Several parties with well-informed guides set out from the parish church in different directions. Dr Nora Acheson (right), in general practice here from 1931 and author of *Up the Steps*, a children's book about Thorpeness and Aldeburgh, is quizzed by Katherine George, a Festival visitor generally accompanied by husband and cat. 1975.

Intrepid visitors on Aldeburgh beach, 1975.

In line abreast in the Aldeburgh Town Walk, Rosamund Strode setting the pace from the middle as they head south along Crag Path, 1975.

Julian Bream, master of the frets, enjoys a jar with friends on Aldeburgh beach, 1975. One of the most frequent Festival performers: on lute, often with partners PP or George Malcolm, or with the Consort that bears his name; on guitar, solo, in the 'Nocturnal' dedicated to him by BB, or with PP in BB's 'Songs from the Chinese' or Walton's 'Anon in Love', all Festival premières; and many other programmes and occasions, including duets with John Williams.

Music on Aldeburgh beach: Hesse students. 1975.

English Chamber Orchestra oboist, James Brown, with conductor and Artistic Director Steuart Bedford, in King Street, Aldeburgh, 1987.

ECO basses, Rodney Slatford and Philip Simms, in rehearsal, 1977.

Steuart Bedford: conductor of the premières of *Death in Venice*, the Folk-Song Suite *A Time There Was*, and the Cantata *Phaedra*. Artistic Director since 1974, he has also played the piano, and conducted concerts and operas, both with the English Music Theatre and the Britten–Pears School. Is there a resemblance here to Joseph Lange's famous unfinished portrait of Mozart? 1977.

Sir William Walton, a frequent visitor to Aldeburgh in Festival time. Having been rather frosty about Britten, he came to have quite an affection and great admiration for him, culminating in his orchestral 'Improvisations on an Impromptu by Benjamin Britten'. His works premièred at the Festival were: 'Anon in Love', written for Peter Pears and Julian Bream and dedicated to one of his hostesses in Suffolk – Lilias Sheepshanks of Eyke – and the comic opera *The Bear* (based on Chekhov). In the photograph WW is writing an inscription to Steuart Bedford on the occasion of *Façade 2*'s first complete performance. 1979.

More leading players of the English Chamber Orchestra – 'house orchestra' of the Festival for many years.

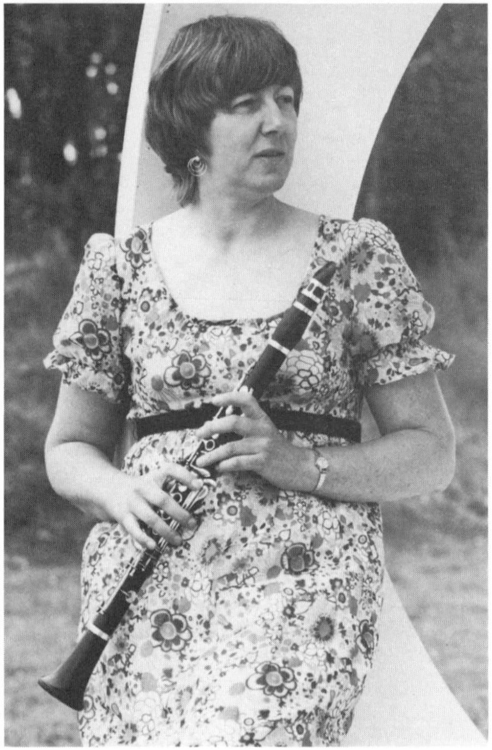

Thea King, a Festival joy since 1961, playing her clarinet – solo, in chamber music or in the ECO, Turning many a Screw, or accompanying Shepherds on Rocks. 1975.

Richard Adeney, another linch-pin of the ECO, has played every kind of flute in every kind of work from concertos to Church Parables. 1986.

James Blades. 'Percussionist Extraordinary'; inventor of percussion-sounds for BB's *The Burning Fiery Furnace* (a Rolls Royce spring as anvil); performer of the J. Arthur Rank gong-strokes and the 'V for Victory' call, broadcast to occupied Europe during World War II. 1979.

Eric Crozier rehearsing Emmie and Cis in the party scene in an excerpt from *Albert Herring*, presented as part of the 70th Birthday Gala for Peter Pears. Harry (Martin Phipps) waits his turn. 1980.

Eric Crozier as Onegin's valet and Richard Jackson as Onegin (Pears sang M Triquet, 'a French tutor') in an unforgettable B–P School production, conducted by Slava Rostropovich to celebrate the centenary of Tchaikovsky's first writing the opera, *for students*: 'Mastery, alas, cannot replace youth', wrote Slava. Impossible to say who was most pleased by this production; conductor, performers or audience. 1979.

Felicity Lott and Richard Jackson, soprano and baritone stars of 'The Songmaker's Almanac'. 1978.

Malcolm Williamson, Australian composer, Master of the Queen's music; at a 50th birthday concert in 1981 he played his piano sonata no. 2; in thirty years, more than a dozen works of his have been performed here, including the première of his opera, *English Eccentrics*. With Sue Phipps, PP's niece and agent. 1981.

Sidney Nolan's paintings of exotic birds, breathtaking as bird-flight, celebrated a lifetime's accomplishment (OM, 1983). Tim Fargher (right), who lives at Orford, has shown only since 1978 – in London and Suffolk. His portraits and landscapes are done with insight and humour: for instance, his line-drawing for Imogen Holst's essay on 'Advantages of being seventy' in the 1980 programme book. 1986.

Bob and Doris Ling: friendliest of concert-hall managers in the building Bob worked in when it was a maltings. Behind them, 1946 posters of the first *Rape of Lucretia*. 1987.

Peter Pears rehearsing with the Wilbye Consort. Elaine Barry, Elisabeth Harrison, Margaret Cable, Ian Partridge and Geoffrey Shaw. 1979.

Jerzy Maksymiuk, Polish conductor and composer, sometime resident in Scotland, here rehearsing the Scottish Chamber Orchestra for the première of 'A Mind of Winter' with the composer George Benjamin on one side and the soprano-soloist Teresa Cahill on the other. 1981.

Cecil Collins, a powerful visionary painter, who has been compared with Chagall. Exhibition in Pears Gallery, 1984.

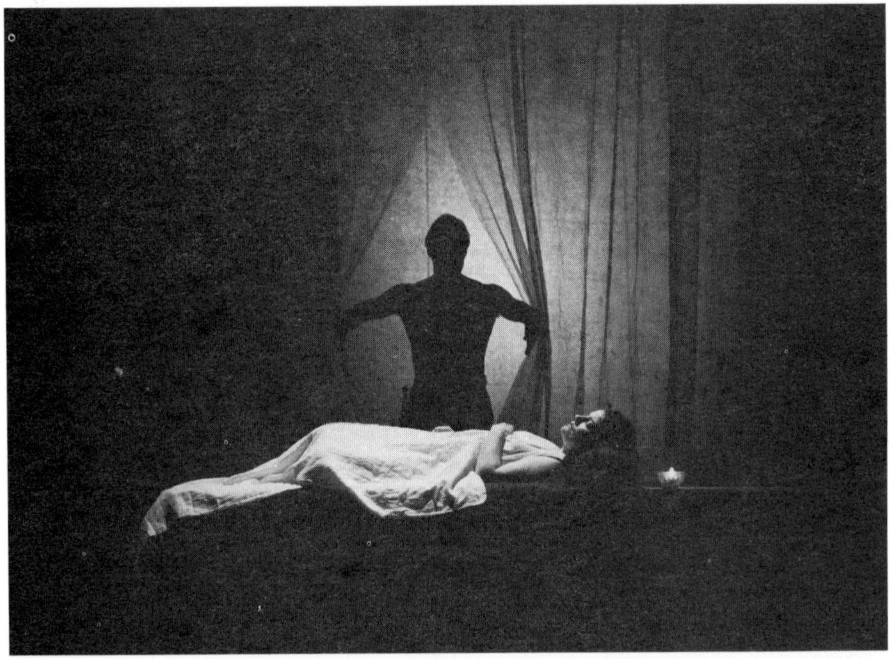

The Rape of Lucretia, Simon Keenlyside (Tarquinius), Barbara Rearick (Lucretia). Maltings, 1987.

Sir Reginald Goodall and Steuart Bedford. Not much Wagner has been heard at the Festival, but Goodall's Act III of *Parsifal* was a revelation. 1987.

Producer and conductor, Basil Coleman and Steuart Bedford, rehearsing *The Rape of Lucretia* simultaneously. 1987.

The Martyrdom of St Magnus by Peter Maxwell Davies. Michael Rippon and Neil Mackie in the Fires of London production in 1979.

The Burning Fiery Furnace, Britten's second parable for performance in Orford church. Abbot, monks and an acolyte prepare to take the parts of the Astrologer (Bryan Drake), Ananias, Misael and Azarias (Glyn Davenport, Paul Whitmarsh and Michael Bauer) and the Angel (Andrew Wigston). 1980.

Edward Fox and Anthony Dowell. EF was Narrator in Honegger's *King David.* AD, Senior Principal dancer of the Royal Ballet, visiting the Festival. 1977.

Sometimes in the Festival, the Joyce Grenfell character talking in between items in the next row would turn round and – what joy! – it *was* Joyce. She's talking here to some of the Hesse students. 1977.

Sylvia Townsend Warner, author of *Lolly Willowes*, *Mr Fortune's Maggot*, dozens of remarkable short stories in the *New Yorker*, also contributions to *Music and Letters* and *Grove's Dictionary of Music*. She and her friend Valentine Ackland 'discovered' John Craske, the Norfolk fisherman-painter (whose work is visible on p. 14). 1977.

Sir Reginald Goodall, who conducted the first performances of *Peter Grimes* in 1945, with Joan Cross, the first Ellen Orford. Joan Cross created many other major roles in Britten's operas, among them the title role in *Gloriana* and the equally imperious Lady Billows in *Albert Herring*. 1986.

Joan Cross with Heather Harper, another Ellen Orford. Heather radiantly created the soprano part in *War Requiem*: it had been written for Vishnevskaya, but Madame Furtseva of the Ministry of Culture would not allow her to sing (1962). 1986.

Blythburgh churchyard on a cool June evening: the New Zealand Dorian Choir sang sacred and secular music, medieval and modern. 1975.

Rosamund Strode, Murray Perahia and Peter Pears arriving – a little late – for George Malcolm's harpsichord recital of Scarlatti sonatas in Blythburgh church, 1985.

The North West entrance to Blythburgh church after the interval between Britten's 1st, and Verdi's only, quartet. Players: Alberni String Quartet. Over the South doorway ahead, ingenious new reconstruction of coloured roof-angel, with the original silver shimmer of medieval tinfoil. 1981.

Bill Servaes with new 1980 programme book outside Blythburgh church. Bernard Levin and Desmond Shawe-Taylor smile with the pleasure that Levin described in the following week's *Listener*. They had just been hearing the first performance of Colin Matthews' 1st quartet played by the Fitzwilliam String Quartet.

Jerzy Maksymiuk, with the Scottish Chamber Orchestra, 1981.

Philip Ledger, 1976.

Imogen Holst, 1977.

Murray Perahia, 1987.

Oliver Knussen, composer, conductor, Artistic Director since 1983, responsible for much of the 20th-century music heard at Aldeburgh, and for the presence 'in residence' of most of the composers we see walking down Crag Path and taking part in the Festivals. Nine of his own compositions have graced the programmes, including two premières. His earliest in 1969, at 16! 1985.

Lutoslawski listens. Delayed at a rehearsal, the distinguished Polish composer stands in the noble South doorway of Orford church awaiting a suitable moment to go in for the tribute to his colleague, Lennox Berkeley. L has paid several visits to the Festival; in 1965 to conduct his *Paroles Tissées*, commissioned and premièred by PP; in 1983, to celebrate his 70th birthday by being Composer in Residence. 1983.

Perahia and Sir Georg Solti (see p. 96). 1986.

The Medici String Quartet, with the composer Jan Carlstedt, whose 4th quartet they performed at Orford, 1986.

Michael Tippett. MT and BB met in 1943; did they ever realise that they were born in places almost equidistant from Aldeburgh, where Sir Michael is seen standing in Britten's garden? When BB was 50, MT dedicated *Concerto for Orchestra* to him; when MT was 60, BB dedicated *Curlew River* to him, at which time BB wrote to him: 'We have been very close often, at other times we have seemed to be moving in different directions. But whenever I see our names bracketed together . . . I am reminded of the spirit of courage and integrity, sympathy, gaiety, and profound musical independence which is yours and I am proud to call you my friend.' Over twenty of MT's works have been performed at the Festival, including the première of his 'Songs for Achilles'. Roebuck sculpted by Georg Ehrlich. 1978.

HM Queen Elizabeth the Queen Mother became Patron of the Festival in 1975 and lunched at the Red House.

Rosamund Strode: musician, writer, many years music assistant, amanuensis and page-turner to Benjamin Britten, and now Archivist and Keeper of the Manuscripts at the Britten–Pears Library. 1975.

A midsummer day's dream amid the bracken, birch and oak that have supplanted heath and sheep along the Sailors' Path was fleetingly diverted by the sight and lingering sound of these woodnymphs and a satyr. Also by the sight of a large treetop heronry. The path was originally beaten by sailors walking between Orford and Aldeburgh via Snape: this warm summer walk from Aldeburgh ended with tea at the Maltings, 1978.

Kenneth Clark (Lord Clark), whose first fifteen years were based on Sudbourne Hall, across the river from Aldeburgh (see p. 9). He delivered master-lectures in the Jubilee Hall and often brought friends to Aldeburgh. 1977.

Thorpeness Meare is part of the holiday and retirement village created by Stuart Ogilvy in the 1920s. Norman Scarfe has helped to row Festival walkers over the Meare to the Boat House, where Alan Powers and Clive Aslet described the creation of the village. 1984.

Near Snape Maltings, a sailing barge – the most beautiful transporter of heavy goods ever created. 1983.

Children are the first to appreciate Henry Moore's sculpture at Snape Maltings. 1975.

Display of falconry at the Maltings, part of the celebration of Peter Pears' 70th birthday. 1980.

Cecil Aronowitz with Imogen Holst; this much-loved musician was, at the Festival for over a quarter of a century, leading the violas of the English Opera Group, Aldeburgh Festival and English Chamber Orchestras. As a chamber music player he was heard in the Melos Ensemble, and as regular 'extra' viola in Mozart quintets with the Amadeus Quartet. As a soloist he gave the first local performances of Shostakovich's late Viola Sonata and the orchestral version of BB's *Lachrymae*. CA was director of strings at the Britten–Pears School and conducted its orchestra until his untimely death. 1977.

Murray Perahia and Clifford Curzon. MP, Artistic Director for seven years, is one of the master pianists of our time. His solo playing is known to the world, but what was special to the Festival was his ensemble work, accompanying PP, playing chamber music with many of his American colleagues, and his piano duets with Sir Clifford Curzon. CC was an old friend of BB, and *they* often played on two pianos. Curzon was also one of the master pianists of his time – a career of nearly sixty years. 1979.

Peter Pears and Oliver Knussen. 1985.

James Burnett, former Music Organiser, BBC Transcription Service, with John Amis. John has a mellifluous tenor voice well known to listeners to *My Music* and his other broadcasts. He has appeared in cabaret at the Festival with prep-schoolmate Donald Swan, and is now a member of the Council of Management. 1984.

Colin Graham reading 'God send patience in our old age' (anon., 15th century) during a performance of works by the great composer of that time, John Dunstable, in Southwold's sublime, steep 15th-century interior. 1976.

The BBC's recording van outside the splendid 15th-century flushwork porch of St Edmund's church, Southwold: the Pendyrus Male Choir, and the Gwent Brass Ensemble performing Liszt's late Requiem for male voices, brass and organ (Huw Tregelles Williams). 1979.

Osian Ellis, Welsh bard and harpist; for him BB wrote and dedicated his Harp Suite. 'How about a harp piece by the young composer from Aldeburgh – BB?' asked Osian. 'Oh, you mean Brendan Brackenthwaite' answered the alternative BB; the première was at the Festival in 1969. OE also played in the Melos Ensemble, with the English Chamber and the London Symphony, and in the première of *A Midsummer Night's Dream* in the Jubilee Hall. 1977.

Osian Ellis, Peter Pears. For their recitals in the 1970s BB wrote Canticle V, 'The Death of St Narcissus', 'A Birthday Hansel' and several folk-song arrangements. 1975.

Elisabeth Söderström, BB, André Previn and PP at a rehearsal of 'Our Hunting Fathers' in 1976.

Arleen Auger, soprano, Jeremy Menuhin, pianist. 1987.

Mstislav Rostropovich, cellist, pianist, conductor, master musician: everything he does seems galvanised by a million volts and informed by the utmost passion. BB wrote five major works for him. Slava loves Aldeburgh, and the love is mutual. 1976.

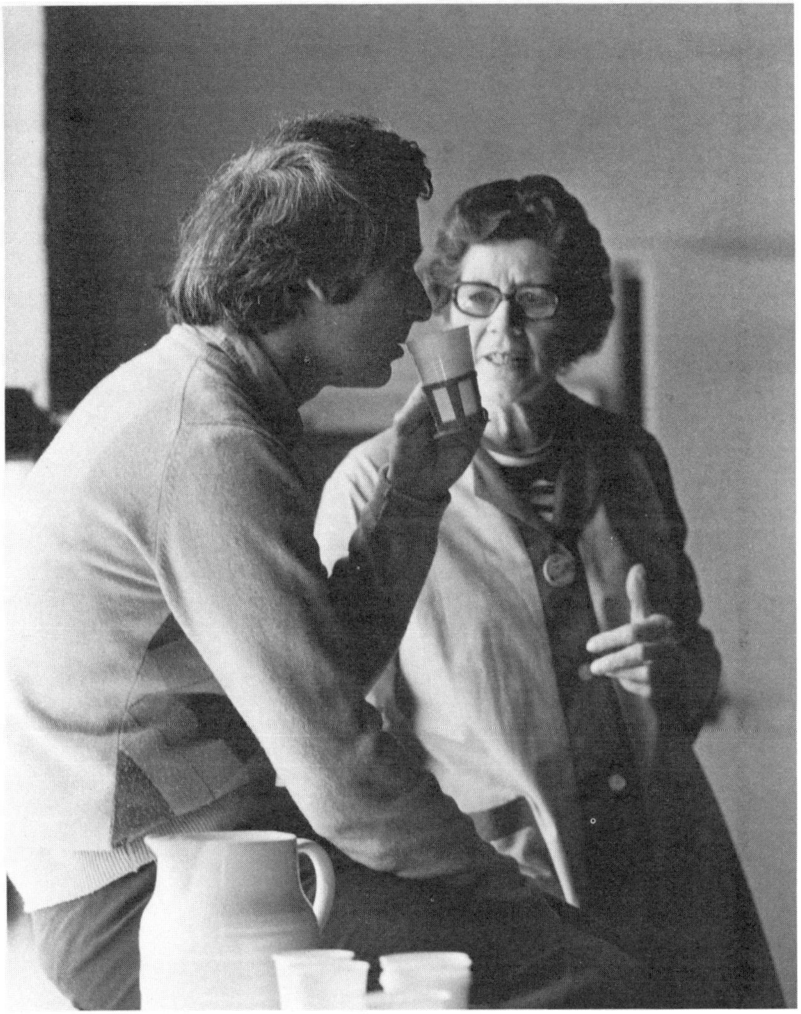

Teabreak. Steuart Bedford and Margot Hare, cheerful manager of the Maltings restaurant. 1977.

Interval drinks: Maltings foyer: Rosamond Lehmann centre stage: the white-fringed hat conceals Lady Diana Cooper. 1977.

Keith Cable with Hesse students on Moot Green, Aldeburgh. A good example of the way the camera captures the casual appearance *and* the essential structure of the town, huddled below the church in two streets running parallel along the line of the seashore. 1976.

Along the High Street at the half-timbered cinema, run indefatigably by Letty Gifford, and one of the most enterprising in the country, George Benjamin accompanies silent films. 1987.

Young composers in the gallery of the Baptist Chapel listening to Eric Crozier's programme, 'Hardy and Music'. Thomas Hardy, George Meredith, Holman Hunt and other distinguished men used to gather each Whitsun at Strafford House on Crag Path, the home of Edward Clodd. 1983.

James Blades showing the next generations how it all works. 1982.

Edward FitzGerald and his music: Handel, Hullah, Last Rose of Summer, Cherry Ripe, Fitz's own songs (including *his* setting of Tennyson's 'The Splendour Falls'), and of course Liza Lehmann's 'In a Persian Garden'. On stage: busts of Tennyson and Hallam at Trinity College, Cambridge, Fitz's own chair and desk from Ipswich Museums, Norman Scarfe (deviser, narrator), Peter Pears, April Cantelo, Rosamund Strode, Steuart Bedford, a grandson of Liza Lehmann. 1977.

Slava Rostropovich accompanying his wife, Galina Vishnevskaya. The soprano is the complete *diva*, unique voice, total command of character and music. Mr and Mrs Rostropovich own a house in Aldeburgh, and sometimes the *diva* can be seen shopping in the High Street. 1978.

Rostropovich with Imogen Holst 1976.

Aldeburgh beach: the *Grimes* element. The Aldeburgh boats carry IH or LT, the registration letters of the ports of Ipswich and Lowestoft. 1986.

Barbara Grayburn's 'box office' at the Jubilee Hall, Aldeburgh. 1986.

Simon Rowland-Jones, Gordon Crosse, and Levon Chilingirian. SR-J was at this time the violist in the Chilingirian String Quartet. The composer Gordon Crosse, an early Hesse student, lives north of Aldeburgh; nine works of his, including three operas, have been premièred at the Festival, a number exceeded by only one other composer(!). The photograph was taken on Crag Path, Aldeburgh, on the first of three Chilingirian visits. 1975.

A Horszowski master class, with Iain Burnside. 1984.

Radu Lupu, whose playing is an amalgam of musical insight, authority, and complete control. He is 'the music while the music lasts'. 1984.

Lupu and Perahia. 1984.

Richard Butt and Robin Holloway. RB has conducted his Birmingham Bach Society choir at the Festival, but his annual presence at a house on Crag Path was mostly through his responsibility for 26 years as senior producer for BBC Radio 3 broadcasting from the Festival. RH, composer, writer of books on music and occasional critic for the *Spectator*. Eight of his compositions have been heard at the Festival, including five premières. The scene is the foyer of Snape Maltings. 1986.

James Galway, flautist, at Snape, with three members of Barbara Hepworth's *The Family of Man*. 1979.

Aldeburgh residents, Mr and Mrs Fairre walking 'Pepper' at Snape. 1975.

To-morrow shall be my dancing day. Imogen Holst watching Morris Men on Moot Green, Aldeburgh. 1977.

Robert Huguenin, who created the role of Tadzio, in daily class in the restaurant bar at Snape.

Tadzio and Aschenbach.

Aschenbach, the most extended role Britten ever created for Pears, was the one in which he made his début at the Metropolitan Opera House, New York, in 1974. Here, towards the end, he stares out over the deserted beach at the Lido.

The Endellion String Quartet rehearsing in Orford church, 1987.

Beth Welford and Adrian Beers at Orford. Beth was born (1909) Elizabeth Britten, the younger of Ben's two sisters; she lived in Aldeburgh till her death in 1989 and wrote a charming book, *My Brother Benjamin*, 1986. Adrian Beers underpinned the Melos Ensemble, and the English Chamber Orchestra, for over twenty years, a Glaswegian double-bass player of international reputation; he played in Schubert's 'Trout' Quintet with Britten at the piano on the disastrous day in 1969 when the Maltings burnt down. The fire consumed both AB and BB's instruments. 1983.

An audience in Orford church has been reflecting on poems and settings of the 1st World War: evening light: font carved c.1400. 1985.

The Orford String Quartet of Canada (Mount Orford) preparing for their concert in Orford church, 1981.

Julian Bream. This master of the lute has been a frequent performer at the Festival. See p. 30. 1987.

The Julian Bream Consort. Playing the 'ancient stave' in Melford Hall: David Sandeman, alto flute; Kenneth Sillito, violin; Jane Ryan, bass viol; Julian Bream, lute; James Tyler, cittern; and Robert Spencer, pandora. 1977.

Loudham Hall was the mid-point in a walk from Rendlesham to Ufford in relentless rain, which explains the stockinged feet: squelchy shoes were left in the kitchen and packed lunches eaten all over the house, all thanks to Angela and Christopher Maclean. The violinist from the B–P School goes well with the distinguished entrance-hall, re-modelled perhaps a little before 1740. 1986.

Christopher Hirons, George Malcolm: violin and harpsichord at Heveningham. GM has been a very frequent visitor to the Festival over the years, playing the piano and organ, conducting choirs, orchestras and opera. He is the dedicatee of Britten's *Missa Brevis* and conducted the first recording of BB's *Cantata Academica*. Heveningham Hall is the most notable example of James Wyatt's works of interior decoration. 1978.

Moira Bennett, Development Director of the Festival, and Rita Thomson, devoted nurse and companion to both Britten and Pears, were at Ickworth House (National Trust), near Bury St Edmunds, for Norman Scarfe's programme about François de La Rochefoucauld's year in Suffolk (1784). It was here at Ickworth that the young Frenchman was much frustrated by the inaccessibility of Lady Bristol's younger daughter. Mary Verney played music of the period on her fortepiano. 1984.

William Bennett and Neil Black, flute and oboe, stalwarts of the English Chamber Orchestra and soloists in their own right. Highlights: 'WIB' tracing Bach through the B minors; and NB vying with Murray Perahia for the greater glory of Wolfgang Amadeus. 1978.

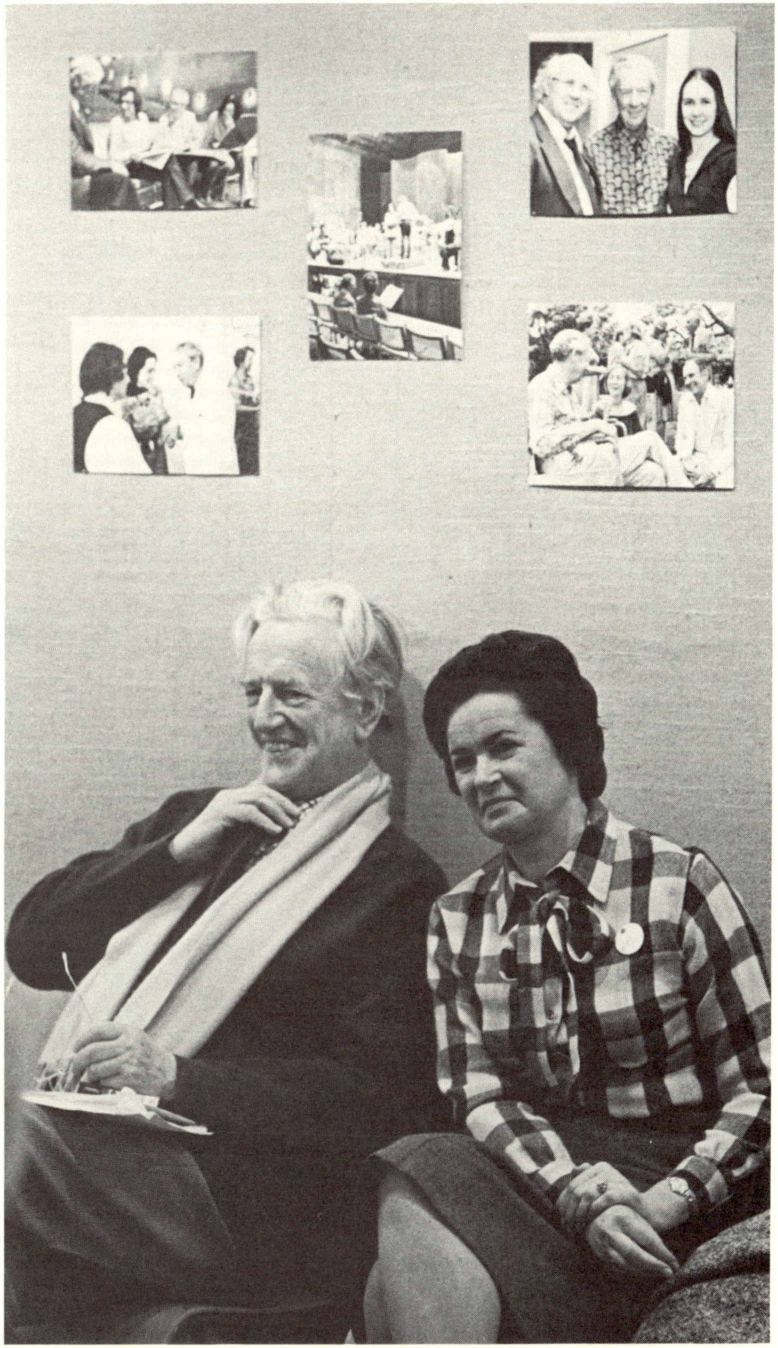

Peter Pears and Marion Thorpe. Herself a pianist, long involved with Fanny Waterman in the great Leeds Prize competition, Marion has been involved in the Festival since the beginning. Daughter of BB's publisher, Erwin Stein and his delightful wife, Sophie. In 1985, her own contribution to the *Tribute* she edited for PP's 75th birthday said everything, including: 'You have made it almost impossible to listen to your repertoire sung by anyone else! You created Ben's works. You inspired composers of younger generations to write for you . . . The privilege of having shared with you and Ben the excitements of planning and achieving so many great musical events goes right back to St Johns Wood High Street days: you and Ben gave shelter to the Steins in 1944 when they had been refugees for the second time – after a fire. Much love, dear Peter.' 1978.

Janet Baker. Dido, Polly, Savitri, Lucretia, Kate, Nuits d'été, Poème de l'amour et de la mer, Wolf, Debussy, Fauré, Argento, Monteverdi – and so the list of Festival memories could continue. The last of them, arguably the most memorable, was Britten's *Phaedra*, written for her in 1975. 1977.

Bill Ewer, master carpenter and builder of platforms, scenery and anything else that's needed, especially at short notice, probably discussing the next 'platform move' with Bert Pearce, 1977.

Hilary Keenlyside (on her front), assistant at the Britten–Pears School and Concerts Manager, helping to repair the backdrop for *Eugene Onegin*, 1979.

John Shirley-Quirk. His roles at the Festival have ranged from Second Servant in Schütz's John Passion via Death (in *Savitri*) and Aeneas through to all seven aspects of the Traveller in *Death in Venice*, that last role composed by BB with J S-Q in mind. Who will ever forget him as the Ferryman in *Curlew River*, or in the *War Requiem*, or 'Journey of the Magi' (all by Britten), not to mention John's Bach, Schubert, Liszt, Wolf, Ravel . . .? 1987.

Imogen Holst's perceptive and constructive comments about music were always treasured by other musicians (this time it is her *own* piece!). With Murray Perahia. 1980.

Richard Pascoe and Princess Grace of Monaco, who took part in 'Theme and Variations', words and music about music. 1978.

Rehearsal for *Phaedra*, 1976. The première of this cantata was on 16th June of that year. Janet Baker – singer/dedicatee; Benjamin Britten – composer; Steuart Bedford – conductor.

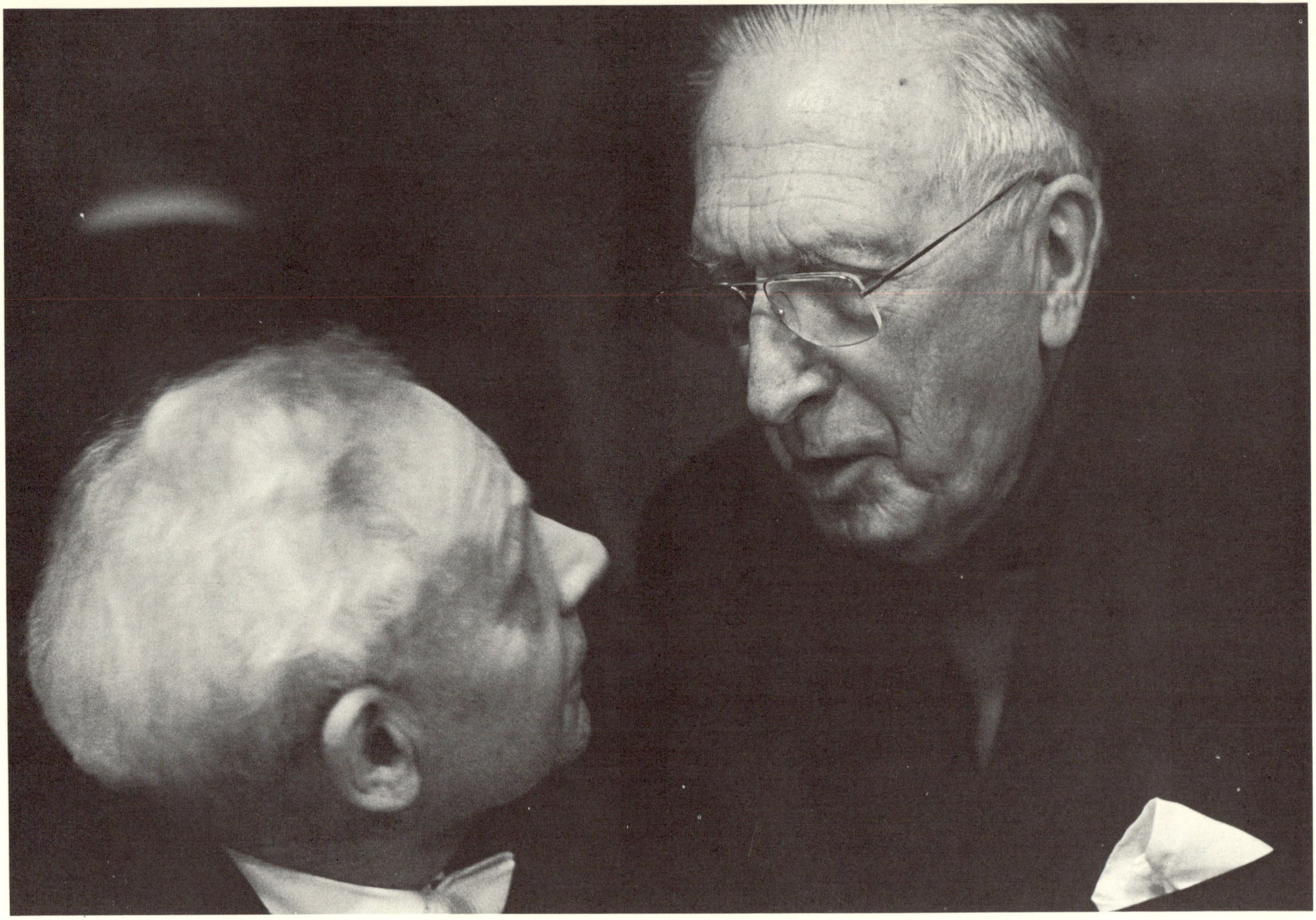

James Blades, William Walton. Putting their heads together in preparation for a performance of *Façade 2*, first complete performance, Snape Maltings. The veteran percussionist – 'hit man' of a hundred Festival appearances with a hundred instruments, some invented specially for the three church parables of BB – and the Lancashire composer were born within a year of each other. 1979.

The composers Robin Holloway and George Benjamin stand on an intact river-bank (or 'wall', as they are called). 1983.

The barge is moored in twilight beside Snape Maltings and in front of the road-bridge that marks the lowest crossing of the Alde's tidal estuary. 1975.

Le five o'clock sur l'herbe. Toru Takemitsu brought some of his exquisite musical enchantments to the Festival as composer in residence, here with Oliver Knussen and Sally Groves, music publisher and daughter to Sir Charles. 1984.

Simon Rattle rehearsing the City of Birmingham Symphony Orchestra for a performance of BB's *Sinfonia da Requiem* in the cathedral at Bury St Edmunds. 1987.

The fluttering departure of the nuns from Henry Moore's sculpture at Snape Maltings has a distant echo of the flight of Carpaccio's monks when St Jerome brought the tame lion into the monastery. 1975.

Monteverdi's great *Vespers of the Blessed Virgin* was sung in her church at Hadleigh, whose rector is also Dean of Bocking so his pinnacled brick house of 1495 is known as the Deanery Towers. Does the line of long-black-skirted and shadowed Festival Singers recall Carpaccio's Venice in the days these towers were new-built? 1986.

Rostropovich with the Snape Maltings Training Orchestra. 1978.

Sir Georg Solti and Charles Kaye. So far (1990) the Hungarian conductor has not directed a symphony orchestra at the Festival but has returned to his first love, the piano, playing duets in 1987 with Murray Perahia; in 1986, with orchestra, each played a Mozart concerto conducted by the other before playing the one for two pianos conducted by both – occasionally at the same time. CK's activities as Sir Georg's secretary run to page-turning. 1987.

Una Incognita, Rosamond Lehmann, and John Ogdon, concentrating. 1976.

Some of the Birds in the production of *Noye's Fludde*, performed by the choir and orchestra of Pimlico school in Orford church, 1978.

Henri Dutilleux, composer in residence, in 1985, at rehearsal with Simon Rattle and CBSO, leader Felix Kok.

Snape Maltings concert hall: the main entrance to the foyer. Unusual to see the grey, lichened asbestos roof 'slates' uncrowned by the four white ventilator-shafts. 1987.

Interval crush in the dramatically vertical old redbrick walled foyer of the Maltings – like a corner of the Baths of Caracalla in Rome. Many 'regulars' are identifiably caught for ever in this photograph. Without resort to the magnifying glass, at least a score are recognised, and others will know others: starting top right and going roughly clockwise – Jeremy Greenwood, Jonathan Griffin, Patrick Trevor-Roper, Sir Lennox Berkeley, Penelope Bray, Lyla Osbiston, Sir Dick Franks, Hugo Herbert Jones, Lady Franks, John Self, Shmuel Ashkenasi, Tom Rochford, Mr Sheffield, Betty Rochford, Margaret Kennedy Scott, Paul Fincham, Rodney and Lady Caroline Blois, Lord Gladwyn, and so on . . . 1985.

Manoug Parikian, solo-violinist and a chamber-music player; he combined both functions memorably at the Festival in Mozart's *Sinfonia Concertante*, the Brahms Double and the Beethoven Triple concertos, also in piano trios with Bernard Roberts and Amaryllis Fleming. 1981.

Ralph and Agnes Downes, and Yehudi Menuhin. 1976 was the first Festival that the musician on the left missed; before that, if anyone was 'seated one day at the organ' it was most likely Ralph Downes, with sometimes four or five appearances a year; after that more rarely (fewer late-night concerts in Aldeburgh church), but Ralph gave a recital in 1984 to celebrate his 80th birthday; and he was there in 1977 with Mrs (Agnes) Downes to hear Yehudi Menuhin play the Elgar concerto. YM has been to the Festival at least half-a-dozen times, playing unaccompanied Bach or Bloch, duos with BB or colleague Alberto Lysy, trios with BB and Maurice Gendron, 'Seasons' *et al.* 1977.

Cynthia Clarey, one of the soloists with the Greenwich Choral Society of Connecticut, 1976.

Marie McLaughlin, as Tatiana in *Eugene Onegin*, 1979.

Roger Norrington. One of his earliest appearances at the Festival was as a tenor with Imogen Holst's Purcell Singers in Byrd's 'Surge, Illuminare' in 1963. Since then RN certainly has 'risen and shone'. Festival devotees will remember his vivid conducting of Schütz, Stravinsky, Schumann's *Manfred* and Monteverdi sacred and profane: the 'Vespers' and 'Orfeo' (with Kent Opera). 1976.

A celebration of Nancy Evans' 70th birthday year. Nancy is talking to Lady Cranbrook, devoted and active chairman of the Festival for many years from its inception, and the Princess Margaret of Hesse, Murray and Ninette Perahia in the background, on the terrace of Blackheath Mansion – Mrs Audrey Vernon-Wentworth's manor house beside the estuary between Aldeburgh and Snape. 1985.

Joan Cross, Sir Lennox Berkeley. Lennox, here characteristically fingering his tie, was an old friend of Ben and Peter's; Peter sang in many performances of LB's beautiful *Stabat Mater* dedicated to BB, already performed twice in the Festival. Five of LB's works have been premièred at the Festival, including the operas *A Dinner Engagement* and *Castaway*. PP presided in 1983 at an 80th birthday tribute to LB. 1976.

Britten's 3rd String Quartet was given its first performance in December 1976, two weeks after the composer's death. This picture was taken at the final rehearsal for that performance by the Amadeus Quartet. Norbert Brainin discusses a point with Imogen Holst. Colin Matthews, on the right, worked closely with Britten during his last years, and since then has worked as editor and adviser on remaining Britten manuscripts.

Ian Brown and Janet Craxton. The pianist is one of the finest chamber music players in the country, featured in many of the performances of the Nash Ensemble. The oboist was a musician much admired by all who heard her, and loved by all who met her. 1980.

Sviatoslav Richter: over the years, unforgettable in Bach, Shostakovich or the ebullient piano concerto of BB, with the composer conducting (1967): most spellbinding of all with BB – four hands at one piano in Aldeburgh church playing Schubert's Fantasia in F minor. Here are two of the hands. 1975.

William Servaes and Sviatoslav Richter in 1975.

Horszowski studied with Leschetitzky, who in turn was taught by Beethoven's pupil, Carl Czerny. 1983.

Alicia de Larrocha (y de la Calle), the distinguished Spanish pianist. 1988.

A piper on the battlements of Framlingham castle: see also Frontispiece. 1975.

Imogen Holst conducting the Band of the Royal Military School of Music, Kneller Hall, at Framlingham Castle on Peter Pears' birthday, 22nd June 1975.

Index to Photographs

IH188